Super Sam

Craig Wright

Name _____

Age _____

Class _____

OXFORD
UNIVERSITY PRESS

OXFORD
UNIVERSITY PRESS

Great Clarendon Street, Oxford OX2 6DP

Oxford University Press is a department of the University of Oxford.
It furthers the University's objective of excellence in research, scholarship,
and education by publishing worldwide in

Oxford New York

Auckland Cape Town Dar es Salaam Hong Kong Karachi
Kuala Lumpur Madrid Melbourne Mexico City Nairobi
New Delhi Shanghai Taipei Toronto

With offices in

Argentina Austria Brazil Chile Czech Republic France Greece
Guatemala Hungary Italy Japan South Korea Poland Portugal
Singapore Switzerland Thailand Turkey Ukraine Vietnam

OXFORD and OXFORD ENGLISH are registered trade marks of
Oxford University Press in the UK and in certain other countries

ISBN-13: 978 0 19 440092 3
ISBN-10: 0 19 440092 1

Printed in Hong Kong

Commissioned photography by: Phil James, *with comic book illustrations by:* Kev Hopgood
Illustrations by: Kev Hopgood

With thanks to Sally Spray for her contribution to this series

To Glenda and family

Reading Dolphins
Notes for teachers & parents

📖 Using the book

1 Begin by looking at the first story page (page 2). Look at the picture and ask questions about it. Then read the story text under the picture with your students. **Use section 1 of the CD for this if possible.**

2 Teach and check the understanding of any new vocabulary. Note that some of the words are in the **Picture Dictionary** at the back of the book.

3 Now look at the activities on the right-hand page. Show the example to the students and instruct them to complete the activities. This may be done individually, in pairs, or as a class.

4 Do the same for the remaining pages of the book.

5 Retell the whole story more quickly, reinforcing the new vocabulary. **Sections 2 and 3 of the CD can help with this.**

6 **If possible, listen to the expanded story (section 4 of the CD). The students should follow in their books.**

7 When the book is finished, use the **Picture Dictionary** to check that students understand and remember new vocabulary. **Section 5 of the CD can help with this.**

💿 Using the CD

The CD contains five sections.

1 The story told slowly, with pauses. Use this during the first reading. It may also be used for "Listen and repeat" activities at any point.

2 The story told at normal speed. This should be used once the students have read the book for the first time.

3 The story chanted. Students may want to chant along with the story.

4 The expanded story. The story is told in a longer version. This will help the students understand English when it is spoken faster, as they will now know the story and the vocabulary.

5 Vocabulary. Each word in the **Picture Dictionary** is spoken and then used in a simple sentence.

This is Todd and Emma.
They are good friends.
They are at Todd's house.
Todd is reading a comic book.

Write. Use these words:

> house   girl   friends   boy
> sofa   comic book

1 Todd is a _boy_ .

2 Emma is a _____ .

3  They are good _____ .

4  They are at Todd's _____ .

5 They are sitting on a _____ .

6 Todd is reading a _____ .

Who is he?

He is my favorite superhero.

What is his name?

His name is Super Sam.
He is the best.

Circle yes or no .

❶ Todd is sitting on a sofa.   (yes) / no

❷ Emma is running.   yes / no

❸ Emma has a comic book.   yes / no

❹ Todd is reading.   yes / no

❺ Super Sam is a superhero.   yes / no

❻ Todd is a superhero.   yes / no

❼ Emma is a superhero.   yes / no

❽ Super Sam is in the comic book.   yes / no

What are these?
Those are his super boots.
What can he do?
He can jump very high
and run very fast.

Trace and number.

blue [3]

orange [ ]

green [ ]

yellow [ ]

boot [ ]

black [ ]

head [ ]

red [ ]

leg [ ]

arm [ ]

white [ ]

brown [ ]

What is this?
That is his flying cape.
Can he fly?
Yes, he can.
He can fly very high.

Circle and answer.

1 What is (this) / these ?

That is his flying cape.

2 What are this / these ?

3 Is / Can he fly?

4 Can he run / jump very high?

5 Who / What is his name?

9

Are these sunglasses?
No, they are his super glasses.
What can he do with them?
He can see through doors
and walls.

Circle yes **or** no .

❶ Super Sam has wings.

yes

(no)

❷ Super Sam can fly.

yes

no

❸ Todd likes Super Sam.

yes

no

❹ Todd has glasses.

yes

no

❺ Super Sam can run very fast.

yes

no

❻ Emma is Todd's sister.

yes

no

❼ Emma can fly.

yes

no

❽ Emma can see through walls.

yes

no

What's wrong?
Super Sam can fly, but I cannot. He can run fast and jump high, but I cannot. I want to be like Super Sam.

Rewrite the sentence correctly.

1 Super Sam is sad.

Todd is sad.

2 Todd can fly.

_____

3 Emma can run very fast.

_____

4 Emma has a comic book.

_____

5 Emma can jump high.

_____

6 Emma wants to fly like Super Sam.

_____

Can Super Sam read a book?

No, he cannot.

Can you read a book?

Yes, I can.

You can read, but he cannot.

Answer the questions.

❶ Can Todd fly?

No, he cannot.

❷ Can Super Sam fly?

_____

❸ Can you fly?

_____

❹ Can Todd read?

_____

❺ Can Super Sam read?

_____

❻ Can Super Sam jump?

_____

❼ Can you read?

_____

Can you write a story?
Yes, I can.
Can Super Sam write a story?
No, he can't. I can write a
story but he cannot.

Circle and write.

❶ (jump) / read   very high

I can *jump very high* .

❷ run / write   a story

I can _____ .

❸ read / fly   a book

I can _____ .

❹ see / run   very fast

He can _____ .

❺ run / fly   very high

He can _____ .

Do you have a computer?

Yes, I do. I like my computer.

Does Super Sam use a computer?

No, he doesn't.

Rearrange the words.

❶ superhero is Super Sam a.

Super Sam is a superhero.

❷ read can a book Todd.

_____

❸ a can story Todd write.

_____

❹ cannot write Super Sam a story.

_____

❺ computer a Todd has.

_____

❻ a computer cannot Super Sam use.

_____

Don't be sad, Todd. Super
Sam can fly, and jump high.
You can read, and write
stories. He has super glasses,
but you have a computer.

Add the missing words.

1 This _is_ Todd.

2 Todd _ _ _ boy.

3 He _ _ _ _ read _ book.

4 He _ _ _ _ _ _ fly.

5 He _ _ _ _ _ computer.

6 This _ _ Super Sam.

7 He _ _ _ _ _ _ _ _ very high.

8 He can _ _ _ _ .

9 He _ _ _ _ _ _ _ _ _ _ _ _ a story.

10 He _ _ _ _ super glasses.

21

You're right!
I can read and I can write.
I can use a computer.
I am not a superhero.
I am a super student!

Answer the questions.

❶ Can you read a book?

_____

❷ Can you use a computer?

_____

❸ Can you write a story?

_____

❹ Can you run very fast?

_____

❺ Do you have super glasses?

_____

❻ Do you like to read comic books?

_____

❼ Are you a super student?

_____

Picture Dictionary

arm  computer

boots  door

cape  fly

comic book  glasses

jump

sofa

leg

wall

read

wing

run

write

Dolphin Readers

Dolphin Readers are available at five levels, from Starter to 4.

The Dolphins series covers four major themes:

Grammar, Living Together, The World Around Us, Science and Nature.

For each theme, there are two titles at every level.

Activity Books are available for all Dolphins.

All Dolphins are available on audio CD.
(2 TITLES ON EACH CD SEE TABLE BELOW)

Teacher's Notes are available at **www.oup.com/elt/dolphins**

	Grammar	Living Together	The World Around Us	Science and Nature
Starter	• Silly Squirrel • Monkeying Around	• My Family • A Day with Baby	• Doctor, Doctor • Moving House	• A Game of Shapes • Baby Animals
Level 1	• Meet Molly • Where Is It?	• Little Helpers • Jack the Hero	• On Safari • Lost Kitten	• Number Magic • How's the Weather?
Level 2	• Double Trouble • Super Sam	• Candy for Breakfast • Lost!	• A Visit to the City • Matt's Mistake	• Numbers, Numbers Everywhere • Circles and Squares
Level 3	• Students in Space • What Did You Do Yesterday?	• New Girl in School • Uncle Jerry's Great Idea	• Just Like Mine • Wonderful Wild Animals	• Things That Fly • Let's Go to the Rainforest
Level 4	• The Tough Task • Yesterday, Today, and Tomorrow	• We Won the Cup • Up and Down	• Where People Live • City Girl, Country Boy	• In the Ocean • Go, Gorillas, Go